What Can H[...]

by Lori Bedoski   **illustrated by Sophia Latto**

Orlando   Boston   Dallas   Chicago   San Diego

Visit *The Learning Site!*

www.harcourtschool.com

ISBN 0-15-325422-X

8 9 10 121 10 09 08 07 06 05 04

Ordering Options
ISBN 0-15-323766-X (Collection)
ISBN 0-15-329541-4 (package of 5)

A cat can not hop.

A pig can not hop.

A ram can not hop.

A snake can not hop.

A bat can not hop.

Can a frog hop?

It can hop!